# STORIES OF ROME

# TARQUINIUS PRISCUS

## SAM VANDERPLAS

**LUCERNA**

This edition published in 2025 by Lucerna Press
Fort Worth, Texas

This work was developed with the assistance of artificial intelligence tools. The content reflects the author's intent and judgment.

ISBN: 979-8-9994863-1-8

Printed in the United States of America

# STORIES OF ROME

# TARQUINIUS PRISCUS

## ADAPTED FROM LIVY

### SAM VANDERPLAS

LUCERNA

King Ancus Marcius was dead.
His sons were nearly grown.
But Tarquinius sent them away,
and assembled the people.
He was the first to seek the crown
with open words and a set speech:

"I came here by choice,
bringing my wife and all I had.
I have lived more years in Rome
than in my native land.
I learned your laws under Ancus,
and served him well in peace and war.
I am no stranger to Rome."

The people elected him king.
The sons returned too late.

Ambition had led him to power,
and it remained on the throne.
He ruled with skill and foresight,
and kept his hold secure.

He named one hundred new senators,
drawn from lesser families.
They owed their seats to Tarquin
and answered to his cause.

The old men kept their places,
and new voices filled the hall.
Rome grew in strength,
as did the king.

Thus Tarquin watched the chamber,
loyal on every side,
strengthening Rome in war and peace,
and guarding his own line.

Tarquin waged his first war
against the Latin town of Apiolae.
He took it by storm and returned to Rome
with spoils beyond all reckoning.

He celebrated with games
in the valley below the hills.
Boxers fought, horns blared, horses raced,
the first great games of Rome.

The knights and senators had wooden seats
around the track's edge.
They were placed on scaffolds,
twelve feet above the dust.

Each year the contests returned,
a feast of speed and sound.
Tarquin had given the people
a spectacle fit for kings.

Tarquin wanted to expand the cavalry
by adding new ranks of horsemen.
But Attus Navius, the chief augur, said
no change could be made without a sign from
the gods.

The king was angry.
He mocked Navius, saying,
"Tell me, you diviner,
can what I'm thinking be done, or not?"

When Navius said it could be done,
Tarquin showed him the test.
"I was thinking you could cut
this whetstone with a razor."

An impossible task.
But Navius took the frail blade
and sliced the stone
into two clean pieces.

From that day on,
the king showed respect for augury.
He made changes to the cavalry
only after the proper signs were given.

The place where the stone was cut
became a mark of wonder.
The people remembered what they had seen,
and spoke of it with awe.

The razor and the whetstone
were buried in that very spot.
A monument was set up nearby,
with Navius shown holding his staff.

From that time forward,
nothing was done without the signs.
Assemblies and armies waited
until the birds gave consent.

Rome fought with the Sabines near a river.
Before the battle, Tarquin sent men in secret
to light firewood on the bank
and float the burning logs downstream.

The wood caught on the bridge,
and soon the whole span was burning.
As the Sabines looked back in fear,
the Roman cavalry struck from both sides.

The Sabines broke and fled,
some over the bridge, some to the river.
Many were killed in battle,
others burned or drowned.

Their shields floated down the river,
reaching Rome before the news.

The Sabines fled toward the hills,
but only a few reached safety.
Most were driven into the river
by the Roman cavalry.

Tarquinius did not rest.
He sent the prisoners and spoils to Rome,
then burned a great pile of weapons
as an offering to Vulcan.

While the enemy still feared him,
he marched into Sabine lands.
The Sabines raised what troops they could
and came out to fight again.

But they were defeated a second time.
They could fight no longer.
They begged the king
to grant them peace.

Tarquin took Collatia from the Sabines
and placed a garrison there.
He left his nephew, Egerius,
to rule the town for Rome.

The people of Collatia surrendered
with a formal vow before the king.
They said they gave up themselves,
their land, their waters, and their gods.

"Do you yield all to Rome?"
asked Tarquin. "We do," they said.
"Then I receive them," said the king,
and peace was made.

Tarquin returned to Rome in triumph.
Soon he marched against the Latins
and conquered many towns,
until all were brought to peace.

Tarquin worked even harder in peace
than he had in times of war.
The people found no rest at home,
only more labor and commands.

He ordered a stone wall
to surround the city completely.
The work had begun before,
but had been halted by the Sabine war.

In the low parts of the city,
near the Forum and the valleys,
he built sloping drains
to carry water into the Tiber.

He also cleared the Capitoline Hill,
to make a level space
for a temple to Jupiter,
as he had vowed in war.

One night in the palace,
a miracle occurred.
A boy named Servius Tullius
lay sleeping, and his head caught fire.

Many saw the blaze,
and cried out in alarm.
A servant ran for water,
but Queen Tanaquil stopped him.

She told them not to wake the boy
until he woke on his own.
When he opened his eyes,
the flame was gone.

Tanaquil took the king aside.
"This child will be a light to us," she said.
"Let us raise him with great care;
he is marked for greatness."

From that day forward,
Servius was raised as a son.
He was taught the ways of the great,
to rule with wisdom and strength.

He grew into a noble man,
with a kingly spirit.
When Tarquin looked for a son-in-law,
no Roman youth could match him.

So the king betrothed his daughter
to Servius, the rising star.
Some said he had been a slave,
but others told a different story.

His mother was noble of birth,
taken when her city fell.
She gave birth in the palace,
and the queen spared her from bondage.

By the thirty-eighth year of Tarquin's reign,
Servius was esteemed by all of Rome.

The sons of Ancus had long resented
the loss of their father's crown.
But now their fury grew,
that the kingdom could pass to Servius.

He was no Roman, not even Italian.
They called him a slave and a son of a slave.
Was Rome to fall so low
after kings descended from gods?

They called it a disgrace to their house,
a stain on the Roman name.
So they resolved,
to stop it with the sword.

The sons of Ancus hated Servius,
but their anger burned hottest against Tarquin.
It was he who stole their crown
and raised a servant to royal heights.

If they murdered Servius,
the king would strike back in fury.
And then, he would still choose
another man to succeed him.

But if the king himself were slain,
there would be no one to avenge him.
The throne would be open,
perhaps even to them.

For these reasons the plot was laid
not against the servant,
but against the king himself.
Tarquinius Priscus must die.

Two of the fiercest shepherds
were chosen for the deed.
They burst into the palace porch,
shouting and shoving like madmen.

Each held the tools of his trade,
a staff and an axe.
They fought so loudly in the entry
that they were called before the king.

Both shouted at once
until a guard ordered silence.
Then, as planned, one began to speak.
The king turned toward him.

At that moment, the other raised his axe
and struck it into the king's head.
They fled,
leaving the king motionless …

## Archaeological Echoes: The Road to Collatia

The stone road pictured here marks the site of ancient Collatia, once a Sabine stronghold and later a Roman town. Tarquinius Priscus conquered it during his campaigns in Latium and placed his nephew in command. The city stood along the Via Collatina, a route that linked Rome with its eastern neighbors. These excavated paving stones, uncovered near modern La Rustica, trace the path Roman soldiers once marched. Though little of Collatia remains above ground, the road itself endures, bearing silent witness to a turning point in Rome's early expansion.

www.ingramcontent.com/pod-product-compliance
Lightning Source LLC
LaVergne TN
LVHW010032070426
835508LV00005B/305